THE MYSTERY OF ENDURANCE

"But he that shall endure unto the end, the same shall be saved."

Mathew 24:13

By
Franklin N. Abazie

The Mystery of Endurance

COPYRIGHT 2018 BY Franklin N Abazie
ISBN: 978-1-945-133-31-2
All right reserved. This book or any portion thereof may not be reproduced or used in any manner whatsoever without the express written permission of the publisher, except for the use of brief quotations in a book review. All Bible quotes are from King James Version and others as noted.

Published by: F N ABAZIE PUBLISHING HOUSE---
a.k.a,
Empowerment Bookstore:

That I may publish with the voice of thanksgiving and tell of all thy wondrous works. **Psalms26:7**

To order additional copies, wholesales or booking: Call the Church office (973-372-7518)
or Empowerment Bookstore Hotline 973-393-8518
Worship address:
343 Sanford Avenue Newark New Jersey 07106
Administrative Head Office address:
33 Schley Street Newark New Jersey 07112
Email:pastorfranknto@yahoo.com
Website www.fnabaziehealingministries.org
Publishing House: www.fnabaziepublishinghouse.org

This book is a production of F N Abazie Publishing House.

A publication Arms of Miracle of God Ministries 2018
First Edition

CONTENTS

THE MANDATE OF THE COMMISSION...........iv

ARMS OF THE COMMISSION............................v

INTRODUCTION..viii

CHAPTER 1

1. How long can I Endure? 27

CHAPTER 2

2. The Reward of Endurance..................................46

CHAPTER 3

3. Prayer of Salvation...65

CHAPTER 4

4. About the Author..73

THE MANDATE OF THE COMMISSION

"THE MOMENT IS DUE TO IMPACT YOUR WORLD THROUGH THE REVIVAL OF THE HEALING & MIRACLE MINISTRY OF JESUS CHRIST OF NAZARETH.

I AM SENDING YOU TO RESTORE HEALTH UNTO THEE AND I WILL HEAL THEE OF THY WOUNDS, SAID THE LORD OF HOST."

ARMS OF THE COMMISSION

1) F N Abazie Ministries-Miracle of God Ministries (Miracle Chapel Intl)

2) F N Abazie TV Ministries: Global Television Ministry Outreach.

3) F N Abazie Radio Ministries: Radio Broadcasting Outreach.

4) F N Abazie Publishing House: Book Publication.

5) F N Abazie Bible School: also called Word of Healing Bible School (W.O.H.B.S)

6) F N Abazie Evangelistic Ass: Miracle of God Ministries: Global Crusade

7) Empowerment Bookstore: Book distribution.

8) F N Abazie Helping Hands: Meeting the help of the needy world wide

9) F N Abazie Disaster Recovery Mission: Global Disaster Recovery.

10) F N Abazie Prison Ministry: Prison Ministry for all convicts "Second chance"

Some of our ministry arms are waiting the appointed time to commence

FAVOR CONFESSION

Father thank you for making me righteous and accepted through the blood of Jesus Christ. Because of that, I am blessed and highly favored by God. I am the subject of your affection. Your favor surrounds me as a shield, and the first thing that people see around me is your favored shield.

Thank you that I have favor with you and man today. All day long people go out of their way to bless me and help me. I have favor with everyone that I deal with today. Doors that were once closed are now opened for me. I receive preferential treatment, and I have special privileges, I am Gods favored child.

No good thing will he withhold from me. Because of Gods favor my enemies cannot triumph over my life. I have supernatural increase and promotion. I declare restoration to everything that the devil has stolen from my life. I have honor in the midst of my adversaries and an increase in assets, especially in real estate and expansion of territories.

Because I am highly favored by God, I experience great victories, supernatural turnarounds, and miraculous breakthrough in the midst of great impossibilities. I receive recognition, prominence, and honor. Petitions are granted to me even by ungodly authorities. Policies, rules, regulations, and laws are changed and reverse on my behalf.

I win battles that I don't even have to fight, because God fights them for me. This is the day, the set time and the designated moment for me to experience the free favor of God, that profusely and lavishly abound on my behalf in Jesus name. Amen.

INTRODUCTION

"And ye shall be hated of all men for my name's sake: but he that shall endure unto the end, the same shall be saved." **Mark 13:13**

I may never get the chance to meet you in person, I am glad you are reading the pages of this small literature. Off course, I cannot tell of your personal trial, and short coming in life. But I do know that God have been your help.

"God is our refuge and strength, a very present help in trouble." **Psalms46:1**

There is nothing in life that we cannot endure, if only we set our mind straight on Jesus. The word says *"Thou wilt keep him in perfect peace, whose mind is stayed on thee: because he trusteth in thee."* **Isaiah26:3**

This small book will help everyone suffering from anxiety, depression, and stress.

The Holy Spirit gave me an insight that will help you endure trials, tribulations, fear, and torment. I do not know your present circumstances but I love to say that God is able.

This small book will inspire you. It is a book of encouragement and motivation, designed to lift up anyone who is depressed, or going through the trials of life. You will agree with me that we all need the spirit of endurance to survive in these desperate times. Come with me together lets hear from the mouth of the Holy Spirit.

Happy Reading!

HIS DESTINY WAS THE CROSS….

HIS PURPOSE WAS LOVE…..

HIS REASON WAS YOU….

"But he that shall endure unto the end, the same shall be saved."

Mathew 24:13

"And ye shall be hated of all men for my name's sake: but he that shall endure unto the end, the same shall be saved."

Mark13:13

"But they that wait upon the Lord shall renew their strength; they shall mount up with wings as eagles; they shall run, and not be weary; and they shall walk, and not faint."

Isaiah 40:31

"And let us not be weary in well doing: for in due season we shall reap, if we faint not."

Galatians 6:9

Endurance Prayer Points

"If ye shall ask any thing in my name, I will do it.." **John14:14**

Holy Spirit of God frustrate and disappoint, every one that is against my life and family, in the name of Jesus.

Father Lord destroy every demonic networks and traps against my progress in life in the name of Jesus.

Fire of God, destroy every demonic projection and curses against my life and destiny in the name of Jesus.

Every spell and curses pronounced against my destiny, break, in the name of Jesus.

Hand of God cage every power militating against my rising in life, in the name of Jesus.

Power of God silent every voice raising a counter motion against my elevation, in the mighty name of Jesus.

Blood of Jesus neutralize every spirit of Balaam hired to hinder my life, ministry, and career, the name of Jesus.

Fire of God destroy every curse that I have brought into my life through ignorance and disobedience, break by fire, in the name of Jesus.

Ancient of day destroy every power harassing my ministry in the name of Jesus.

Father God deliver me from invincible forces militating against my life and destiny.

Power of God frustrate every coven and demonic network, designed to frustrate and hinder my success in life, in the name of Jesus.

I dismantle every strong hold designed to imprison my talent in the mighty name of Jesus.

I reject every cycle of frustration, in the name of Jesus.

Power of God paralyze every agent assigned to frustrate my life in the name of Jesus.

Finger of God, grant me supernatural speed against all my contenders in the name of Jesus.

By the blood of Jesus, I destroy every familiar spirit caging my life and career.

Fire of God arrest every demonic agents, assigned to police my destiny and marriage.

By the blood of Jesus, I proclaim no weapon fashioned against me shall ever prosper.

Holy Spirit of God break me through and forward in life in the mighty name of Jesus.

God, smash me and renew my strength, in the name of Jesus.

Holy Spirit, open my eyes to see beyond the visible to the invisible, in the name of Jesus.

Father Lord grant me strength and power in the name of Jesus.

O Lord, liberate my spirit to follow the leading of the Holy Spirit.

Holy Spirit, teach me to pray through problems instead of praying about, it in the name of Jesus.

Father Lord, deliver me from the false accusation in life, in the name of Jesus.

By the blood of Jesus, every evil spiritual padlock and evil chain hindering my success, be roasted, in the name of Jesus.

By the blood of Jesus I rebuke every spirit of spiritual deafness and blindness in my life, in the name of Jesus.

Father Lord, empower me to dominate the enemy of my destiny in the name of Jesus.

Jesus Christ of Nazareth, heal my infirmities in the name of Jesus.

Lord, anoint my eyes and my ears that they may see and hear wondrous things from heaven.

Father Lord, anoint me with power and authority to dominate all my enemies in the name of Jesus.

Fire of God roast every giant rising up against my life and career.

Holy Spirit of God destroy all my oppressors in the name of Jesus.

Angels of good new, bring my good news to me in the mighty name of Jesus.

Every strong man holding me down, lose your hold now in the name of Jesus.

I nullify every demonic prediction over my life in the name of Jesus.

By the blood of Jesus, I flush out every polluted deposit of the enemy in my life.

By the blood of Jesus, I paralyze every enemy of my promotion in the name of Jesus.

Father Lord, destroy any power tormenting my life that is not from you.

Holy Ghost fire, ignite the fire of revival in my life.

By the blood of Jesus, I declare victory over every conflicting trial.

By the Blood of Jesus, I command the arrest of every demonic spirit, militating against my life .

By the blood of Jesus, I proclaimed the blood of Jesus, over every device of the enemy.

By the blood of Jesus, I revoke stagnation and hardship over my life in the name of Jesus.

Holy Ghost fire, destroy every satanic arrangement in my life, in the name of Jesus.

Circular problems, assigned to my life, you will not prosper, backfire, in the name of Jesus.

Every satanic project, against my breakthrough, explode in the face of the enemy, in the name of Jesus.

Every dream of backwardness, go back to your senders, in the name of Jesus.

Any power, working round the clock, with dark powers, against my life, perish, in the name of Jesus.

Every household Cain, assigned to waste my Abel, you will not succeed, rush to your grave and die, in the name of Jesus.

Every domestic enemy, anointed by Satan, to terminate my life, terminate your own life, in the name of Jesus.

Anti-Christ power of my father's house, assigned to punish me, die, in the name of Jesus.

Every satanic contact of my father's house, hunting for my life, die, in the name of Jesus.

Every magician, astrologer and diviner, assigned against me, go back to your senders, in the name of Jesus.

Every evil progress, against my life, perish, in the name of Jesus.

Mid-night and mid-day arrows, fired at me, collide on the Rock of Ages and backfire, in the name of Jesus.

Every giant, occupying my promised land, lose your hold, in the name of Jesus.

By the power that silenced Sennacherib, I silence my adversaries forever, in the name of Jesus.

Every wicked altar, harboring my name and my picture, collide with thunder and die, in the name of Jesus.

Every affliction, targeted at me, explode in the hands of your owners, in the name of Jesus.

Every king Saul of my household, pursuing my David, die, in the name of Jesus

Satanic grave digger of my father's house, dig your own grave and enter into it, in the name of Jesus.

Any power that has joined witchcraft and occult group to attack me, thus saith the Lord, suffer not a witch to live, lose your life for my sake, in the name of Jesus.

Arrows of shame, disgrace, and mockery, fired into my life, backfire, in the name of Jesus.

Arrows of rise and fall, fired at me, expire, in the name of Jesus.

Every vulture of darkness, assigned to eat my flesh, go back to your senders, in the name of Jesus.

Every verdict of darkness, issued against me, backfire, in the name of Jesus.

Every dominant wicked power of my father's house, I bury you now, in the name of Jesus.

Every satanic traditional manipulation, assigned to remove my glory, fail, in the name of Jesus.

Any power, assigned to make me irrelevant in my generation, your time is up, die, in the name of Jesus.

Any power, giving me a deadline to die, fall down, and die on your own deadline, in the name of Jesus.

Every strange material and strange deposit, in my body, disappear now and go back to your senders, in the name of Jesus.

Every satanic payroll, where my enemies registered my name, I delete my name and substitute it with the names of the enemies, in the name of Jesus.

Any wicked hand, collecting evil against me, decay, and die, in the name of Jesus.

By the power that silenced Haman in favor of Mordecai, O Lord, let every power assigned against my existence, die, in the name of Jesus.

Any power assigned to manipulate my destiny, enough is enough, scatter, in the name of Jesus.

Every assembly of the wicked, delegated to destroy my destiny, scatter, in the name of Jesus.

Every ancient strongman, laboring to waste my efforts, my life is not your victim, expire, in the name of Jesus.

Every wicked mouth, sowing evil seeds against me, I command the seeds to catch fire, in the name of Jesus.

Every ancient gate, standing against my breakthroughs, scatter, in the name of Jesus.

I plug my destiny, into the mystery of divine favor, in the name of Jesus.

O thou that troubled the Israel of Miracles of God Ministries, the God of Elijah shall trouble you today.

Every enemy, of the Miracles of God Ministries, scatter, in the name of Jesus.

O God, arise and uproot anything You did not plant inside the Miracles of God Ministries, in Jesus' name.

You fire of revival, fall upon Miracles of God Ministries, in the name of Jesus.

CHAPTER 1
How long can I Endure?

"But he that shall endure unto the end, the same shall be saved." **Mathew24:13**

"And let us not be weary in well doing: for in due season we shall reap, if we faint not." **Galatians 6:9**

I have always had to answer the above question numerous times. Often church folks ask me, how long will I go through this? Or how long can I endure this? Jesus said *"Thou therefore endure hardness, as a good soldier of Jesus Christ."*

It is written, *"These things I have spoken unto you, that in me ye might have peace. In the world ye shall have tribulation: but be of good cheer; I have overcome the world."* **John16:33**

It is written, *"But the fruit of the Spirit is love, joy, peace, longsuffering, gentleness, goodness, faith"* **Gal5:22**

Most of us tend to forget that endurance is among the fruit of the spirit. Longsuffering also means endurance. In the Greek language, the term for patience is often translated *"long-suffering"*. It's a compound word. The first part means *"long or far"*.

The second part means *"hot, anger, or wrath"*. Putting it together we literally have *"long-anger"*. We have an English expression *"short-tempered"*. We would not miss the meaning very far if we called patience *"long-tempered"*. Patience is that ability that keeps us from blowing up when events don't go our way or losing our cool when others upset us.

As long as we live we must face challenges. A great man of God said what you fail to confront you cannot conquer.

Chapter 1 - How long can I Endure?

Endurance simply means - *the ability to hang on when all hope is lost*. Endurance simply means fighting the fight of faith in the midst of the storms, and adversaries of life.

Most of us are blessed in life with other significant attributes, like speed of accomplishment, good health, and excellent wives/husbands.

Just a number of us can go through longsuffering in this technology age that we live in. I have read news of suicide for simply things like bullying, fear, and resentment. As an African- coming from Nigeria, we easily adapt and adjust to any prevailing circumstance in life. *"Quitters never win and winners never quit."*

For instance, I came a mighty long way to ever think of anything in life that will steal my joy. God brought me out, when I had nothing, God will see me through to have something in life. May that become your mentality in the Mighty Name of Jesus. If you must not give up easily in life, you need to develop the spirit of endurance in life.

Endurance simply means accepting Jesus in our life. Looking up to the cross and not to the world. We came with nothing, we shall definitely leave with nothing.

It is written, *"Wherefore, if God so clothe the grass of the field, which today is, and tomorrow is cast into the oven, shall he not much more clothe you, O ye of little faith?"* **Mathew6:30**

"Therefore take no thought, saying, What shall we eat? or, What shall we drink? or, Wherewithal shall we be clothed?" **Mathew6:31**

"And said, Naked came I out of my mother's womb, and naked shall I return thither: the Lord gave, and the Lord hath taken away; blessed be the name of the Lord." **Job1:21**

A great example of a great man who endured colossal financial lose in life is the man called Job. The bible recorded that Job lost his entire business empire. Yet he did not commit suicide. The bible says that *"In all this Job sinned not, nor charged God foolishly."* **Job1:22**

Chapter 1 - How long can I Endure?

In this part of the world people give up easily. I really need to take you on a week journey to Nigeria- West Africa, for you to see for yourself how other people are living yet rejoicing and happy. How people will give testimonies for the slightest thing that happened in their life. Most people in America have no testimony because they expect God to spoon feed them.

"Give glory to the Lord your God, before he cause darkness, and before your feet stumble upon the dark mountains, and, while ye look for light, he turn it into the shadow of death, and make it gross darkness." **Jer13:16**

How long can I endure?

For unless endurance becomes our lifestyle we will forever be filled with anxiety and worry in life. I love for you to engraft it into your mind, that endurance is a continual thing. As long as we live will endure hardship.

"Thou therefore endure hardness, as a good soldier of Jesus Christ." **2timothy2:3**

Life is full ups and downs, obstacles that are predictable and un-projectable. It is my prayer that you embrace the spirit of endurance as a believer. Endurance simply is the key victory in life.

Endurance *"the power of pushing forward despite prevailing obstacles and challenges in life"*. Popular colloquial phrases describe it as: *"Keep on keeping on"*. *"Hang in there." "Put up with it." "Stick-to-itiveness." "Don't quit."* Its synonyms are determination, perseverance, tenacity, plodding, stamina, and backbone.

Often whenever endurance is used in the Bible it means *"to abide under," "to bear or put up courage,"* and *"to tarry or wait."*

The Bible considers endurance a priority. It is a significant part of our daily living as believers. *"Many are the afflictions of the righteous: but the Lord delivereth him out of them all."* **Psalms 34:19**

Chapter 1 - How long can I Endure?

Apostle Paul admonished timothy strongly to develop the spirit of endurance.

"Thou therefore endure hardness, as a good soldier of Jesus Christ." **2timothy2:3**

"Cast not away therefore your confidence, which hath great recompence of reward." **Hebrew10:35**

"For ye have need of patience, that, after ye have done the will of God, ye might receive the promise." **Hebrew10:36**

How do I to develop the spirit of endurance?

I. We must accept the things we cannot change in our lives

We must embrace and accept those things in our lives that we cannot change.

Please take a few minute and pray this prayer out loud.

Father God, grant me the serenity to accept the things I cannot change; courage to change the things I can; and wisdom to know the difference.

Living one day at a time; enjoying one moment at a time; accepting hardships as the pathway to peace; taking, as He did, this sinful world as it is, not as I would have it; trusting that He will make all things right if I surrender to His Will; that I may be reasonably happy in this life and supremely happy with Him forever in the next. **Amen**.

William Barclay described endurance as *"the courageous acceptance of everything life can do to us and the transmitting of even the worst event into another step on the upward way."*

The truth is, things happen in life. There are circumstances that are inevitable. We have no control over it. Sometimes, life is not fair if I may say it that way. Injustices creep into every one's life at one point or the other.

Chapter 1 - How long can I Endure?

It helps for everyone to remember that God is in charge of our lives. His desire is for us to grow in the likeness of His image. So whatever happens to our life - unfavorable circumstances, tragic events, death, or abusive people –it is for the maturity of our moral character. Be it good, bad, or indifferent our response to life's irritants mold and shape our personality.

J. B. Phillips understood this as he paraphrased **James 1:2-4**: *"When all kinds of trials crowd into your lives, my brothers, don't resent them as intruders, but welcome them as friends! We must realize that those events test our endurance. But let the process go on until that endurance is fully developed, and you will find out, you have become men and women of matured character."*

II. Adapt and adjust to prevailing circumstances

Sometimes we have to adjust our way to fit the realities of life. Solomon wrote, *"A sensible person sees danger and takes cover, but the inexperienced keep going and are punished"* **Prov. 22:3**.

Often, there are circumstances are unavoidable. Disappointments will always kick in, some unforeseen circumstances may oppose us. Obstacles are sure. Losses will occur. I encourage you to develop the spirit of endurance, acknowledge obstacles in your life, and make appropriate adjustments.

Are you allowing intrusions to distort and disfigure your life? Are their circumstances or people in your life that you have been trying to change the outcome of your life? As faithful believer, never allow such circumstances to overtake your life. I pray God, may help come for you from above in Jesus Mighty Name.

When we adjust to the detours of life God reveals some of his marvelous handiwork off the beaten trail. Don't think of adjustment as failure, think of it as an education. Hang on, see what God has in store for you around the next bend in the road.

Chapter 1 - How long can I Endure?

III. Abide with patience

Someone once said, *"You can do anything if you have patience. You can carry water in a sieve - if you wait until it freezes."* Unfortunately, most of us aren't that patient. When we need it, we usually pray, *"Lord, give me patience . . . and I want it now."* Or, as Margaret Thatcher, former British Prime Minister, said more eloquently, *"I am extraordinarily patient provided I get my own way in the end."*

But one can't learn patience by listening to a sermon unless the sermon is so long they have to practice it while they listen. Nor can they learn patience by reading a book unless the book is so boring that they have to muster up patience to finish it. The only way to learn patience is by facing this hurly-burly world, taking life as it comes. It is holding on, gritting your teeth, clinching your jaw, riding out the storm.

And that is not easy. Joyce Landorf writes, *"God's waiting room is the most difficult aspect of the Christian experience."*

Believers are exhorted to display patience. James wrote, *"Therefore, brothers, be patient until the Lord's coming. See how the farmer waits for the precious fruit of the earth and is patient with it until it receives the early and the late rains. You also must be patient. Strengthen your hearts, because the Lord's coming is near"* **James 5:7-8**.

James shows how the farmer demonstrates patience. A farmer cannot make it rain or give growth. He must rely on God to act in the most wise and merciful way.

The secret of patience is abiding. We must learn to rest and endure under the load of pain and suffering. We abide under the load of pain and suffering by abiding with a God who is faithful. We must not only learn to abide in Christ but also abide with Christ under the struggles and the pressures in life.

Chapter 1 - How long can I Endure?

IV. Affirm the presence

As we progress toward a life that resembles Jesus Christ we must always remember that God is with us. Sometimes God is like a teacher instructing us with the construction. Sometimes God is a fellow-worker challenging us to excellence.

Sometimes God is a spectator encouraging us to keep on keeping on. Whatever situation we find ourselves, God is always with us.

Isaiah described this miracle: *"Do you not know? Have you not heard? Yahweh is the everlasting God, the Creator of the whole earth. He never grows faint or weary; there is no limit to His understanding. He gives strength to the weary and strengthens the powerless. Youths may faint and grow weary, and young men stumble and fall, but those who trust in the LORD will renew their strength; they will soar on wings like eagles; they will run and not grow weary; they will walk and not faint"* **Isaiah 40:28-31 NIV**

The secret is found in affirming God's presence. The world says give up, drop out, run away. God says to just trust me, lean on me, and fall into my arms. God is with you to support and sustain you. To give you hope, courage, and strength to continue. He has promised, *"My presence will go [with you], and I will give you rest"* **Ex. 33:14**.

In our quest for contagious character, unpolished and incomplete though we may be, it is the Master who surrounds us and whispers in our ear, time and again, *"Don't quit - keep playing."*

And as we do, he augments and supplements until a work of amazing beauty is created. What we can accomplish on our own is hardly noteworthy. We try our best but the results aren't exactly graceful flowing music. But with the hand of the Master, our character can truly be beautiful. Our responsibility is to not quit, to keeping playing; his part is to fashion a masterpiece.

Chapter 1 - How long can I Endure?

Remember God doesn't call the equipped. He equips the called. And, he'll always be there to love and to guide you to great things.

In summary

Are you close to quitting? Please don't do it.

Are you frustrated, and tired of trying to live for Christ? Hang in there and pray.

Do you feel like giving up on the Christian life? Join a prayer group and get back to God.

Can't resist temptation? Accept God's forgiveness and keep on living rightly.

Do you feel that sorrow and disappointment greet your every morning? Hold on. Help is just around the corner.

Endurance prevails. *"Blessed is a man who endures trials, because when he passes the test he will receive the crown of life that He has promised to those who love Him"* **(Jas. 1:12 NIV)**. Remember you are not a failure until you give up trying in life. You are not a flop until you let go.

So don't quit. Never give up. Keep going. Hold on. God's rewards await us in the distant future not near the beginning; and we don't know how many steps it will take to reach the prize. No breaks or time outs exist; we must work every day of our life.

It has been said, *"Life is like reading a book. It begins to make sense when we near the end."* Endurance maintains the stamina needed to see the end and embrace the prize. So fight another round, rise another time, and, above all, like don't let go.

2 Corinthians 6:4-10

"But in everything commending ourselves as servants of God, in much endurance, in afflictions, in hardships, in distresses."

Chapter 1 - How long can I Endure?

Hebrews 10:32

"But remember the former days, when, after being enlightened, you endured a great conflict of sufferings."

Hebrews 12:3

"For consider Him who has endured such hostility by sinners against Himself, so that you will not grow weary and lose heart."

Revelation 2:3

"And you have perseverance and have endured for My name's sake, and have not grown weary."

Romans 5:3-4

"And not only this, but we also exult in our tribulations, knowing that tribulation brings about perseverance."

James 1:2-4

"Consider it all joy, my brethren, when you encounter various trials."

Hebrews 10:32

"But remember the former days, when, after being enlightened, you endured a great conflict of sufferings."

Hebrews 12:3

"For consider Him who has endured such hostility by sinners against Himself, so that you will not grow weary and lose heart."

Revelation 2:3

"And you have perseverance and have endured for My name's sake, and have not grown weary."

Romans 5:3-4

"And not only this, but we also exult in our tribulations, knowing that tribulation brings about perseverance."

James 1:2-4

"Consider it all joy, my brethren, when you encounter various trials."

Chapter 1 - How long can I Endure?

James 1:12

"Blessed is a man who perseveres under trial; for once he has been approved, he will receive the crown of life which the Lord has promised to those who love Him."

Romans 12:12

"Rejoicing in hope, persevering in tribulation, devoted to prayer."

CHAPTER 2
The Reward of Endurance

"And ye shall be hated of all men for my name's sake: but he that shall endure unto the end, the same shall be saved." **Mark 13:13**

"But he that shall endure unto the end, the same shall be saved." **Mathew 24:13**

"Cast not away therefore your confidence, which hath great recompence of reward." **Hebrew 10:35**

Everything in life has its season and timing. Often everyone is hurrying to get the blessing right now. But there is always a due season in life. The word of God says *He will fulfil the desire of them that fear him:*

"For ye have need of patience, that, after ye have done the will of God, ye might receive the promise." **Hebrew 10:36**

"Blessed are ye, when men shall revile you, and persecute you, and shall say all manner of evil against you falsely, for my sake." **Mathew5:11**

"Rejoice, and be exceeding glad: for great is your reward in heaven: for so persecuted they the prophets which were before you." **Mathew5:12**

As a business man, your business will experience profit and loss, ups and down at one point. But it takes the spirit of endurance to survive, and succeed.

As a pastor, your ministry will gain and lose membership, you may suffer from accommodation and financial short coming, but it takes endurance to survive and succeed in ministry.

We need the spirit of endurance in every aspect of life. *"Rome was not built in a day."* If you must succeed in your life, you must pray for the spirit of endurance.

Chapter 2 - The Reward of Endurance

"For our light affliction, which is but for a moment, worketh for us a far more exceeding and eternal weight of glory." **2cor4:17**

"For his anger endureth but a moment; in his favour is life: weeping may endure for a night, but joy cometh in the morning." **Psalms30:5**

I pray for you to develop the spirit of endurance.

"Endurance: It is the spirit which can bear things, not simply with resignation, but with blazing hope. It is the quality which keeps a man on his feet with his face to the wind. It is the virtue which can transmute the hardest trial into glory because beyond the pain it sees the goal."

Endurance is when you don't give up on hardships and continue working towards the goal in spite of the hardships.

Endurance, a single word with a powerful meaning.

The word is used in both contexts of philosophy and also in terms of exercise. It basically means that you have to stay focused and continue the journey in spite of thousands of obstacles. The obstacles are going to be there in various forms, but you have to make sure that you don't back out.

Anything is possible, but all it needs is some more endurance from your side to go ahead and do it.

Below is a compilation of some great quotes which might be spiritual in some sense, or might be about how you have to carry on if you're an athlete and excel in your chosen sport. Some might even seem funny, but they'll make you fall in love with the idea of enduring. Do not just read them, but also try to remember them for life.

Quotes on Endurance

"Endurance is one of the most difficult disciplines, but it is to the one who endures that the final victory comes." — **Gautama Buddha**

Chapter 2 - The Reward of Endurance

"What cannot be altered must be borne, not blamed." — **Thomas Fuller**

"Not in achievement, but in endurance, of the human soul, does it show its divine grandeur and its alliance with the infinite." — **Edwin Hubbel Chapin**

"Endurance is patience concentrated." — **Thomas Carlyl**

"I know quite certainly that I myself have no special talent; curiosity, obsession and dogged endurance, combined with self-criticism have brought me to my ideas." — **Albert Einstein**

The Importance of the Spirit of Endurance

1. Endurance gives hope, and courage: Anything you start in life, needs time to mature and grow. Endurance gives us hope and courage.

2. Endurance releases faith: Although life is full of uncertainty, endurance gives us the faith to keep up. It is faith that will lead anyone into victory:

3. Endurance gives us experience in life: You do not know anything until you have been through something in life. We are faced with uncertainty especially in new terrain in business or ministry. The spirit of endurance grants us the experience that is relevant for our survival.

4. The spirit of endurance makes us stronger and tougher. If you must emerge stronger and tougher, you must crave for the spirit of endurance in life.

5. If only you can endure the pains, you will enjoy the gains. The psalmist said weeping may endure for a night, but joy cometh in the morning.

No matter where you find yourself in life, strive to endure. Do not give up for winner never quit. Life is full of ups and downs, I pray God turn your life around for good in the mighty Name of Jesus.

Chapter 2 - The Reward of Endurance

CONCLUSION

"Cast not away therefore your confidence, which hath great recompence of reward." **Hebrew10:35**

"For ye have need of patience, that, after ye have done the will of God, ye might receive the promise." **Hebrew10:36**

No one can endure the trials and tribulations of life if they do not know Jesus. Until you encounter Jesus Christ, you are not set or deliverance. To become a new creature means to carry the traits and spirit of endurance.

"Therefore if any man be in Christ, he is a new creature: old things are passed away; behold, all things are become new." **2cor5:17**

What must I do to determine my divine visitation?

To determine divine visitation you must be born again. The word says as many as received him, to them gave He power to become the sons of God. Even to them that believe on his name.

To qualify for divine visitation do the following sincerely;

1) Acknowledge that you are a sinner and that He died for you. **Rom3:23**.

2) Repent of your sins. **Acts 3:19, Luke13:5, 2Peter3:9**

3) Believe in your heart that Jesus died for your sin. **Romans10:10**

4) Confess Jesus as the Lord over your life. **Romans10:10, Acts2:21**

Chapter 2 - The Reward of Endurance

Now repeat this Prayer after me

Say Lord Jesus, I accept you today, as my Lord and my savior, forgive me of my sins wash me with your blood. Right now, I believe, I am sanctified, I am save, I am free, I am free from the Power of sin to serve the Lord Jesus. Thank you Lord for saving me. Amen.

I adjure you to watch the Spirit of God bear witness with your Spirit confirming His word with signs following. The word says The Spirit itself beareth witness with our spirit, that we are the children of God. Join a bible believing church or join us on our weekly and Sunday worship services at 343 Sanford Avenue Newark New Jersey 07106.

WISDOM KEYS

Every Productive Society is a society heading to the top

Millions of Nigerians run away from Nigeria, very few Nigerians stay in Nigeria.

My decision to return Nigeria is the will of God for my life

My short coming in America after 18 years, trained me to be wise, to think, reflect and reason appropriately.

If you train your mind to reason it will train your hands to earn money.

It is absurd to use the money of the heathen to build the kingdom of the living God.

Every Ministry reveals its agenda and goal either at the beginning or at the end. Be careful of your life it is your first Ministry.

The average American mind is conditioned for a continual quest to get new things and (discard the former) and throw away old things.

Chapter 2 - The Reward of Endurance

When I considered well, my BMW jeep became my initial deposit for the work of the ministry in Nigeria

Everyone is waiting for you to change your mind until you change your thinking nothing changes around you.

Multiple academic degrees in other discipline gave me the chance to think, reflect and reason

What so everyone are thinking and reflecting at the moment reveals you to the time and the now factor

All events and intents are the product of precise thought processes, accurate reason every event is designed for a designated timeline

Wisdom is your ability to think, to create and invent. If you can think wise enough you will come out of penury

The distance between you and success is your creative ability to think reason and reflect accurate.

Success is the result of hard work, commitment resolve and determination learning from past mistakes and failing.

If you organize your mind you have organized your life and destiny.

There is a thin line between success and failure. If you look above and beyond you are on your way to success.

Wealth is your ability to think, power is your ability to reason and success is your ability to be informed.

If you can make use of your mind by thinking and reasoning God will make use of your life and destiny.

Think and Be Great

Reflect, Reason, think and be great

Famous people are born of woman

Chapter 2 - The Reward of Endurance

That you will make it is your intention; that you will survive is your resolve, that you will succeed with changes is your determination, personal efforts and hard work.

No man was born a failure. Lack of vision is the end product of failure.

Working with mental patients encourages and aspire me to be a productive observant and dedicated to my assignment.

Successful people are not magicians, it is the will power combined with hard work, and determination and a resolve to succeed that make them succeed.

In the unequivocal state of the mind, intention is not a location or a position it is the state of the mind.

So many people think that they think. The mind is used to think reflect and reason. You will remain blind with your eye open until you can see with your mind by thinking.

There is no favoritism in accurate and precise calculation

Although knowledge is power, information is the key and gateway to a great future.

It will take the hand of God to move the hand of man.

With the backing of the great wise God, nothing will disconnect you from your inheritance.

As long as you have wisdom and understanding of God, Satan and evil cannot manipulate your life and destiny.

You have come this far by yourself judgment and decision you have made in the past, now lean and listen to God for another dimension of greatness.

Great people are common people it is extra ordinary effort and the price of sacrifice that produces greatness.

As a mental direct care worker I saw a great pastor and a motivational speaker within myself.

Menial job does not reduce your self-worth, until you resolve to achieve greatness see greatness in all you do; you will never count in your community

Chapter 2 - The Reward of Endurance

The principle of Jesus will solve your gambling and addiction problems

The man of Jesus will lead you into heaven,

Everyone have their self-appraisal and what they think about you. Until you discover yourself other opinion about you will alter the real you.

Supervisors and directors are just a position in the chain of command in a work place. Never allow your supervisor hierarchy to alter your opinion about yourself.

Everyone can come out of debt if they make up their mind.

That I am not a decision maker at work does not diminish my contribution to my world.

Although it appears like it was a poor decision to accept a direct care employment at a psychiatric hospital as I reflect of my nine years of experience, it became apparent that I have learnt and experienced enough for my next assignment.

Self-encouragement and determination is a resolve of the heart.

If you are determined to make a difference, and do the things that make a difference you will eventually make a difference.

Good things do not come easy

Short cuts will cut your life short.

Those who look ahead move ahead.

Life is all about making an impact. In your life time strive to make an impact in your community.

Make friends and connect with people who are moving ahead of you in life.

If you can look around well you have come a long way in your life, made a lot of difference and realized a lot of success in life.

If you are my old friend, hurry up to reach out to me before I become a stranger to you.

Everything I am blessed with inspirations from God, that change my definition and interpretation of the world around me.

I thought I was stagnant and lonely until I looked around and noticed my children running around and my wife cooking.

Chapter 2 - The Reward of Endurance

At 40 I resigned my Job to seek the Lord forever.

My ministry took a drastic rise to the top when the wisdom of God visited me with knowledge and understanding.

You will be a better person if you understand the characteristics of your personality – your mood swings attitudes and habits.

It is the seed of love you sow into the heart of a child and a woman that you reap in due time.

Love is not selfish, love share everything including the concealed secrets of the mind.

As long as you have a prayer life and a bible; you will never feel lonely, rejected and idle in the race of life.

When good friends disconnect from you, let them go, they might have seen something new in a different direction.

Confidence in yourself and in God is the only way to bring you out of captivity

Never train a child to waste his/her time.

The mind is the greatest assets of a great future.

The Mystery of Endurance by Franklin N. Abazie

You walk by common sense run by principles and fly by instruction.

Those who fly in flight of life fly alone.

Up in the air you are alone. No one can toll you accept the compass of knowledge and information

I have seen a tolling vehicle I have seen a tolling ship I have never seen a tolling airplane.

I exercise my judgment and make a decision every minute of the day.

Decisions are crucial, critical and vital with reference to your future.

So many people wish for a great future. You can only work towards a great future.

Your celebrity status began when you discovered your talent. What are you good at? Work at it with all commitment.

Prayers will sustain you but the wisdom of God will prosper you.

When I met Oyedepo, his teachings changed my perspective, but when I met Ibiyeomie; His teaching changed my perception.

The Mystery of Endurance by Franklin N. Abazie

I will be successful in ministry if only I concentrate and focus my energy in the work of the ministry.

It took the late Dr. Vincent Pearle Norman's book to open my mind towards kingdom success.

CHAPTER 3
PRAYER OF SALVATION

I am glad you have read this book all the way from the beginning to this point. All I have said from the beginning will remain a mystery until you commit it into practice.

And before you do so I want you, if you have not given your life to Jesus to do so now. Give your life to Christ. I want you to know the truth! The truth is that Jesus died for your sins and because He died you must be alive and prosperous.

What must I do to determine my salvation?

To be saved we must be born again! The word says as many as received him, to them gave He power to become the sons of God. Even to them that believe on his name.

To qualify for divine visitation do the following sincerely,

1) Acknowledge that you are a sinner and that He died for you. **Rom3:23.**

2) Repent of your sins. **Acts 3:19, Luke13:5, 2Peter3:9**

3) Believe in your heart that Jesus died for your sin. **Romans10:10**

4) Confess Jesus as the Lord over your life. **Romans10:10, Acts2:21**

Now repeat this Prayer after me

Say Lord Jesus, I accept you today, as my Lord and my savior, forgive me of my sins wash me with your blood. Right now, I believe, I am sanctified, I am save, I am free, I am free from the Power of sin to serve the Lord Jesus. Thank you Lord for saving me. Amen.

I adjure you to watch the Spirit of God bear witness with your Spirit confirming His word with signs following. The word says The Spirit itself beareth witness with our spirit, that we are the children of God.

Chapter 3 - Prayer of Salvation

MIRACLE CARE OUTREACH

"...But that the members should have the same care one for another" **1cor12:25**

We are all members of the body of Christ. Jesus commanded us to love our neighbor as ourselves. This includes caring for one another as a member of one body. True love is expressed in caring and giving. The word says for God so Love He gave….

Reach out to someone in need of Jesus, help someone in crisis find Christ. Look out and prove your love to Jesus by caring and inviting your friends and associates to find Jesus the Healer.

Invite your friends to our Home Care Cell Fellowship (Miracle chapel Intl Satellite fellowship) In the USA at 33 Schley Street Newark New Jersey 07112.

If you are in Nigeria—**MIRACLE OF GOD MINISTRIES**

A.K.A"MIRACLE CHAPEL INTL" Mpama –Egbu-Owerri Imo state Nigeria.

(Home Care Cell fellowship Group). We meet every Tuesday at 6:00pm-7:00pm.

LIFE IS NOT ALL ABOUT DURATION BUT ITS ALL ABOUT DONATION

What does the above statement mean?....

"Life consists not in accumulation of material wealth.." **Luke12:15.**

"But it's all about liberality....meaning- what you can give and share with others." **Proverb11:25.**

When you live for others--You live forever- because you out live your generation by the legacy you live behind after you depart into glory to be with the Lord. But when you live to yourself - you are reduced to self—you are easily forgotten when you die and depart in glory.

Permit me to admonish you today to live your life to be a blessing to a soul connected to you today.

Chapter 3 - Prayer of Salvation

I want you to know that so many souls are connected and looking up to you, and through you so many souls will be saved and rescued from destruction. Will you disciple someone today to find Jesus Christ?

"As a genuine Christian; it is your duty to evangelize Jesus Christ to all you meet on your way. Jesus is still in the healing business-Jesus is still doing miracles from time of old to now.

Therefore tell someone about Jesus Christ today, disciple and bring them to Church."

John 1:45 Philip findeth Nathanael....

Please to prove the sincerity of your love for God today; please become a soul winner. The dignity of your Christianity is hidden in your boldness to proclaim and evangelize Jesus Christ to all you meet on your way.

There is a question mark on the integrity of your Christianity until you become a life soul winner. Invite someone to join us worship the Lord Jesus this coming Sunday.

MIRACLE OF GOD MINISTRIES

PILLARS OF THE COMMISSION

We Believe Preach and Practice the following,

1) We believe and preach Salvation to every living human being

2) We believe and preach Repentance and forgiveness of sins

3) We believe and preach the baptism of the Holy Spirit and Spiritual gifts

4) We believe and teach the Prosperity

5) We believe and preach Divine Healing and Miracles (Signs &Wonder)

6) We believe and preach Faith

7) We believe and Proclaim the Power of God (Supernatural)

8) We believe and Proclaim Praise& Worship to God

Chapter 3 - Prayer of Salvation

9) We believe and preach Wisdom

10) We believe and preach Holiness (Consecration)

11) We believe and preach Vision

12) We believe and teach the Word of God

13) We believe and teach Success

14) We believe and practice Prayer

15) We believe and teach Deliverance

This 15 stones form the Pillars of Our Commission.

Become part of this church family and follow this great move of God.

MY HEART FELT PRAYER FOR YOU

It is my prayer that you develop the spirit of endurance in the mighty Name of Jesus Christ.

Now let me Pray for you:

Father I thank you for giving me the spirit of endurance. Lord God of heaven grant me the courage and the fortitude to survive any prevailing obstacle ragging against my life and destiny. I give you thanks in advance. In Jesus Mighty Name.

Amen.

CHAPTER 4
ABOUT THE AUTHOR

Rev Franklin N Abazie is the founding and Presiding Pastor of Miracle of God Ministries with headquarters in Newark, New Jersey USA and a branch church in Owerri- Imo State Nigeria. He is following the footsteps of one of his mentors, Oral Roberts (Healing Evangelist) of the blessed memory.

The Lord passed Oral Roberts healing mantle two days before he went to be with the Lord at age 91 into the hand of healing evangelist-Rev Franklin N Abazie in a vision.

In all his services the Power and Presence of God is present to heal all in his audience. He is an ordained man of God with a Healing Ministry reviving the healing and miracle ministry of Jesus Christ of Nazareth.

Pastor Franklin N Abazie, is called by God with a unique mandate:

"THE MOMENT IS DUE TO IMPACT YOUR WORLD THROUGH THE REVIVAL OF THE HEALING & MIRACLE MINISTRY OF JESUS CHRIST OF NAZARETH.

I AM SENDING YOU TO RESTORE HEALTH UNTO THEE AND I WILL HEAL THEE OF THY WOUNDS. SAID THE LORD OF HOST"

He is a gifted ardent Teacher of the word of God who operates also in the office of a Prophet, generating and attracting undeniable signs & wonders, special miracles and healings, with apostolic fireworks of the Holy Ghost.

He is the founding and presiding senior Pastor of this fast growing Healing ministry.

He has written over 86 inspirational, healing and transforming books covering almost all aspect of divine healing and life. He is happily married and blessed with children.

BOOKS BY REV FRANKLIN N ABAZIE

1) Commanding Abundance
2) The outcome of faith
3) Understanding the secret of prevailing prayers
4) Understanding the secret of the man God uses
5) Activating my due Season
6) Overcoming Divine Verdicts
7) The Outcome of Divine Wisdom
8) Understanding God's Restoration Mandate
9) Walking in the Victory and Authority of the truth
10) Gods Covenant Exemption
11) Destiny Restoration Pillars
12) Provoking Acceptable Praise
13) Understanding Divine Judgment
14) Activating Angelic Re-enforcement
15) Provoking Un-Merited Favor
16) The Benefits of the Speaking faith
17) Understanding Divine Arrangement

18) Understanding Divine Healing
19) The Mystery of Endurance
20) Obeying Divine Instructions
21) Understanding the Voice of God
22) Never give up on Hope
23) The prevailing Power of faith
24) Understanding Divine Prosperity
25) The Reward of Prayer
26) Covenant Keys to Answered Prayers
27) Activating the Forces of Vengeance
28) Put your faith to work
29) Where is your trust?
30) The Audacity of the Blood of Jesus
31) Redeeming Your Days
32) The force of Vision
33) Breaking the shackles of Family Curses
34) Wisdom for Marriage Stability
35) Overcoming prevailing challenges
36) The Prayer solution
37) The power of Prayer
38) The Effective Strategy of Prayer
39) The prayer that works
40) Walking in Forgiveness
41) The power of the grace of God

42) The Power of Persistence
43) Overcoming Divine verdicts
44) The audacity of the blood of Jesus.
45) The prevailing power of the blood of Jesus
46) The benefit of the speaking faith.
47) Fearless faith
48) Redeeming Your Days.
49) The Supernatural Power of Prophecy
50) The companionship of the Holy Spirit
51) Understanding Divine Judgement
52) Understanding Divine Prosperity
53) Dominating Controlling Forces
54) The winners Faith
55) Destiny Restoration Pillars
56) Developing Spiritual Muscles
57) Inexplicable faith
58) The lifestyle of Prayer
59) Developing a positive attitude in life.
60) The mystery of Divine supply
61) Encounter with the Power of God
62) Walking in love
63) Praying in the Spirit
64) How to provoke your testimony

65) Walking in the reality of the Anointing
66) The reality of new birth
67) The price of freedom
68) The Supernatural power of faith
69) The intellectual components of Redemption
70) Overcoming Fear
71) Overcoming Prevailing Challenges
72) My life & Ministry
73) The Mystery of Praise

MIRACLE OF GOD MINISTRIES
NIGERIA CRUSADE 2012

MIRACLE OF GOD MINISTRIES
NIGERIA CRUSADE 2012

MIRACLE OF GOD MINISTRIES

NIGERIA CRUSADE

2012

MIRACLE OF GOD MINISTRIES

NIGERIA CRUSADE

2012

www.ingramcontent.com/pod-product-compliance
Lightning Source LLC
Chambersburg PA
CBHW021448080526
44588CB00009B/740

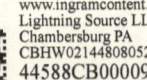